Praise for This Book

Kathleen Nielson has written a book that will improve your prayer life for your children. As you read *Prayers of a Parent for Adult Children*, you can feel the love, compassion, concern, and wisdom of a mother who has thoughtfully prayed for her own children and those of others for years. It is a beautiful expression of how to guide others to Christ while expressing the love Christ has for his own. This book will help parents grow closer to Christ as they pray for their offspring.

—**Miguel Núñez and Catherine Scheraldi-Núñez**, Senior Pastor and Director of Women's Ministries, International Baptist Church, Santo Domingo

Praise for the Prayers of a Parent Series

We love how these beautiful, biblical prayers help us to "pray most earnestly" (1 Thess. 3:10), to "pray without ceasing" (1 Thess. 5:17), and to pray specifically for our own children. Furthermore, pastors should encourage every member to pray for the children of the church and assist them in doing so. This book would be a huge help to that end, for often people are willing to pray but "do not know what to pray for" (Rom. 8:26). For those in congregations that take vows to assist parents in the Christian nurture of their children, we can't imagine a better or more important way of fulfilling their vows than praying for those children from their youth onward.

—**Anne and Ligon Duncan**, Wife, Mother, Christian Educator; Chancellor and CEO, Reformed Theological Seminary

I know of no greater gift that a parent can give to their child than the gift of prayer centered on the gospel. That's why I'm so excited about this project from Kathleen Nielson. Filled with faith, hope, and love, each prayer is accompanied by relevant

Scripture and a focused exhortation to help any parent put into words what they long for in their hearts. Having prayed for and with our two daughters for the last two decades, my wife and I look forward to using it!

—**Julius J. Kim**, President, The Gospel Coalition

Kathleen Nielson has coupled scriptural truth with beautifully crafted poetic prayers that bring hope. As a mom, I am encouraged to consider afresh the many ways I must pray for my children. Kathleen helps me with the joyful task by lifting my eyes upward, creating a Word-focused mission of intercession. As a parent (whether natural or spiritual), you too will be challenged in the prayers you pray—prayers that are bound to change not only your children's hearts but yours as well.

—**Blair Linne**, Author; Speaker; Spoken Word Artist

Kathleen Nielson understands the longings of our hearts for the spiritual flourishing of our children. She gives these longings beautiful and Bible-shaped expression. A treasure for every Christian parent!

—**Dane C. Ortlund**, Author, *Gentle and Lowly: The Heart of Christ for Sinners and Sufferers*

There is no greater joy for Christian parents than to hear that their children are walking in the truth. But how do we pray toward that end, day in and day out, through every stage of their lives? I can think of no better guide than this series by Kathleen Nielson—a diligent student of God's Word, a wonderful writer, and a praying mother (and now grandmother). Because these prayers are so Scripture saturated, you can have confidence that you are praying in accord with the will of our good and sovereign God. Take up and read, and pray, and by God's grace you could change your world.

—**Justin Taylor**, Managing Editor, *ESV Study Bible*

Since as parents we have no ability whatsoever to change the hearts of our children, prayer for them is not a spiritual luxury; it is essential. It is an amazing grace to us that God welcomes, hears, and answers our prayers. I know of no other guide to parental prayer like Nielson's tender, insightful, gospel-rich, and loving little book. Read it and you will find yourself praying for new things for your children in new ways than you have before, and as you do, you will grow in affection for your Father and in how you approach him in prayer.

—**Paul David Tripp**, Author, *New Morning Mercies: A Daily Gospel Devotional* and *Parenting: 14 Gospel Principles That Can Radically Change Your Family*

Parenting is important and hard. How do you pray through this complexity? What do you pray when you aren't sure what to say or how to say it? Kathleen Nielson knows the parental spiritual roller-coaster. She's lived it. And prayed through it. This book will give you words to pray and encouragement to ponder as you navigate the issues and challenges of real-world parenting. It helped me. I think it will help you as well.

—**Mark Vroegop**, Lead Pastor, College Park Church, Indianapolis; Author, *Dark Clouds, Deep Mercy: Discovering the Grace of Lament*

Prayers of a Parent
for Adult Children

Prayers of a Parent Series

Kathleen Nielson

Prayers of a Parent for Young Children
Prayers of a Parent for Teens
Prayers of a Parent for Young Adults
Prayers of a Parent for Adult Children

Prayers of a Parent
for Adult Children

Kathleen Nielson

P&R
P U B L I S H I N G
P.O.BOX 817 • PHILLIPSBURG • NEW JERSEY 08865-0817

Scripture quotations are from the ESV® Bible (The Holy Bible, English Standard Version®), copyright © 2001 by Crossway, a publishing ministry of Good News Publishers. Used by permission. All rights reserved.

Italics within Scripture quotations indicate emphasis added.

Printed in the United States of America

Library of Congress Cataloging-in-Publication Data:

Names: Nielson, Kathleen Buswell, author.
Title: Prayers of a parent for adult children / Kathleen Nielson.
Description: Phillipsburg, New Jersey : P&R Publishing, [2021] | Series: Prayers of a parent | Summary: "Adult children will always need the love and support of their parents and their God. Lift them up with short, poetic prayers to our heavenly Father who hears and answers"-- Provided by publisher.
Identifiers: LCCN 2021008939 | ISBN 9781629958262 (paperback) | ISBN 9781629958279 (epub) | ISBN 9781629958286 (mobi)
Subjects: LCSH: Parents--Prayers and devotions. | Adult children--Prayers and devotions. | Adult children--Religious life. | Parent and adult child--Religious aspects--Christianity.
Classification: LCC BV4529 .N54 2021 | DDC 242/.645--dc23
LC record available at https://lccn.loc.gov/2021008939

For our three sons,
and their three beautiful wives, now like daughters,
and our grandchildren, eight so far—
what amazing gifts from God.
I love praying for you!

Contents

Introduction

How being a parent makes one pray—through the years! Our adult children need our prayers. As we parents long to encourage and help them, prayer is no last resort. Our prayers are perhaps the most important way to help our children as they move on in life. Our prayers focus our own hearts before God, and they lift up our children to the heavenly Father who hears us, and who answers according to his perfect will. How amazing to think that Christian parents can keep reaching out in prayer to God our Father, who has shown his love to us in his own Son—and who gives us his Holy Spirit to help us pray, according to his Word.

These prayers have grown from my heart through years of praying for three sons—and now for their growing families. I know that you parents (and grandparents, and aunts and uncles, and spiritual mothers and fathers!) will surely pray for your children in your own words and with your own specific praises and petitions. My hope is that these prayers might mingle profitably with yours, as we all lift up the next generations to the Lord who knows and loves them perfectly.

These prayers grow out of the Scriptures; each is printed

with a brief related Bible passage and reflects that passage in its content. What confidence, that when we don't know how to pray for our children, the Spirit and the Word guide and help us. Just as the Scriptures show us Jesus Christ at the very center, so these prayers aim to focus on Jesus—his love, his work of salvation on our behalf, his glory, his blessed rule in every area of our lives, his coming again.

The prayers apply to sons and daughters both; they alternate, but any of them can easily be changed by switching the pronouns appropriately. Please note: the prayers are written in one parent's voice, although they can certainly be prayed by parents together. Parents, please know that these prayers, as they focus on our children, inevitably focus often on us parents too. Prayer stretches our hearts in all kinds of ways.

Let us pray!

Kathleen Nielson

As for man, his days are like grass;
  he flourishes like a flower of the field;
for the wind passes over it, and it is gone,
  and its place knows it no more.
But the steadfast love of the LORD is from everlasting to
    everlasting
on those who fear him,
  and his righteousness to children's children,
to those who keep his covenant
  and remember to do his commandments.
The LORD has established his throne in the heavens,
  and his kingdom rules over all. (Ps. 103:15–19)

There's nothing like having adult children to help make clear just how quickly life moves on, generation after generation. It is humbling and good to watch the next generation take their places. It makes us pray indeed.

May we wrap these prayers all around with worship to the Lord who rules history and watches over his people forever. The world changes, and we change, but God's redemptive love in Jesus Christ his Son does not change: "Jesus Christ is the same yesterday and today and forever" (Heb. 13:8).

Of Worship and Trust

I look up to you, O Lord of all,
and see your everlasting greatness,
bow before your heavenly throne.
As I bow low, I see our fleetingness,
our human days that sprout like grass, and grow,
and then are gone.

I thank you that your steadfast love
will never cease, but is
from everlasting past to everlasting future
on the ones who fear you;
and your righteousness will not run out,
but extends farther than we can see—
to children's children.

I humbly pray, O Father God,
that you would spread your love
to generations, in and through my child,
displaying your great gift of righteousness
in this next human life, and then another,
all passed on by your redeeming grace,
received by faith in your redeeming Son,
as your regenerating Spirit brings new life.

Through generation after generation,
may praise keep on rising to your throne,
until the Day when all of us will gather round it,
shining like the Son,
and never parting, never ceasing
praise and worship to you, glorious Lord.

But we are not of those who shrink back and are destroyed, but of those who have faith and preserve their souls.

Now faith is the assurance of things hoped for, the conviction of things not seen. For by it the people of old received their commendation. By faith we understand that the universe was created by the word of God, so that what is seen was not made out of things that are visible. (Heb. 10:39–11:3)

The book of Hebrews gives us a picture of God's people through the ages pressing forward in faith, believing God's Word. In Old Testament times, God gave promises of things yet to come, and his faithful people lived in the assurance of things hoped for: they trusted his Word.

The fulfillment of all God's promises bursts into sight with the coming of Jesus, his death on the cross, and his resurrection from the grave. We believers continue to live now in faith, looking back to the cross and the empty tomb, looking up to the glorified Christ in heaven, and looking forward to his promised coming again.

Let's pray that our children would be of those who press forward in faith, by God's grace, believing God's Word and assured of the hope of Christ's glorious return.

Through a doorway: see Revelation 4–5.

For Faith

May my child walk on in faith,
with eyesight ever clearer for the things not seen—
invisible realities that draw believers forward
with a hope that only grows with passing years.

Lord Jesus, may he see you
as just through a doorway—
Lamb of God who died, now risen, glorious,
interceding there at God's right hand
for the ones who are your own by faith,
the gift of your amazing grace.

May those around him sense not fading dreams
or shrinking spirit; may he ever more clearly grow
in strength of soul, whether his body is weak or strong.
May he exude conviction of those things not seen,
so others are convicted, too, to look, and see.

When doubts arise, or doubters challenge,
may he turn always to your powerful Word.
By your word, Lord God, the universe was made—
the seen made out of unseen, from the start.
Please let him trust your Word so mercifully revealed,
so fully shown to us in Christ your Son, our Savior.
Please let your Word sustain and grow his faith,
through every moment on the way to full and perfect sight.

May he walk on through life in faith,
with eyesight ever clearer for the things he's yet to see.

15

These are written so that you may believe that Jesus is the Christ, the Son of God, and that by believing you may have life in his name. (John 20:31)

You may know very personally the pain of watching a child wander, without faith in Christ. We ache for these children.

And we pray. Even as our hearts ache, we pray. For these wanderers we pray—and nothing makes us pray more, often persisting through years of petition, not knowing the answer to our prayers.

As we pray, we come to grasp the comfort and the power of prayer to the Lord who sees into every heart. In these prayers, we learn to rest in what we know—or *whom* we know, the sovereign and loving Lord of all.

Your breathed-out Word: see 2 Timothy 3:15–16.

For a Wanderer

Bdd

Lord God, I do not know and cannot see her heart,
but all her steps appear to turn away from you,
away from light and life found in your Son.

I know, Lord, that you see into the darkest heart;
your perfect wisdom lays out all our paths.
Please turn her feet and move her heart
toward you, toward life in Christ, I pray.

I do not know just how you might ordain
to call her to yourself to find eternal life
and life abundant, through believing in your Son.

I know that you have given your breathed-out Word,
the writings that can make us wise for salvation
as we believe that Jesus is the Christ, the Son of God,
the living Word made flesh to save us.
Please, by your Spirit and your people,
speak your Word of life into her heart, I pray.

I do not know the ways in which her story will unfold,
or how your perfect purposes will guide her path.

I know with thankful heart
that you have sent your Son to give us life.
I know you, Lord, and live in you.
I trust in you, even as I daily ask,
please lead her to believe in Christ your Son, I pray.

Teach me, O Lord, the way of your statutes;
and I will keep it to the end.
Give me understanding, that I may keep your law
and observe it with my whole heart. (Ps. 119:33–34)

In most cases, words of parents to grown children are far fewer than they were to growing children. We don't speak to and with them quite as much—but we speak to the Lord about them just as much!

And we ask God continually that it would be his voice, his Word, to which our grown children would be listening. The inspired Scriptures are God's own breath to us humans; we need his breathed-out Word to live on by faith. Our children need this Word.

We can't always talk about this with our children, especially adult ones. But we can trust God's Word, pray according to it, and pray that our children would *keep* it, as the psalmist prays, now and to the end.

For Word Habits

Keep him, Lord, and may he keep your Word—
learning and delighting in its truth;
trusting in the Savior there revealed;
repenting when he falls and fails to heed your voice;
seeking help and strength to put his faith to work;
humbly hearing other saints who teach him well;
humbly teaching others what you've let him learn;
guarding your inspired words, not adding or taking away;
praying for your Spirit to give understanding;
praying, too, for a soft heart to trust and to obey;
worshiping with gathered saints around your Word;
singing songs that celebrate your truth revealed;
confessing sins together as the Bible sheds its light;
taking care to hear your voice in all the Scriptures;
discovering your glorious Son on every page;
grasping your redemptive plan from the beginning;
following well the unfolding prophetic word;
glorying in the Gospels as they show us Jesus in the flesh;
stopping long, again, again, to see the cross where Jesus died;
believing resurrection truth, and knowing resurrection power;
digging into the Epistles' doctrine and the call to live it out;
refusing to adjust your truth, for peace or ease;
telling the good news near and far, so others can believe;
studying the hope to come, and living looking for Jesus's return.

Keep him, Lord, and may he keep your Word;
by your grace please let him keep it to the end.

If then you have been raised with Christ, seek the things that are above, where Christ is, seated at the right hand of God. Set your minds on things that are above, not on things that are on earth. For you have died, and your life is hidden with Christ in God. When Christ who is your life appears, then you also will appear with him in glory. (Col. 3:1–4)

We humans never finish struggling with issues of identity. Especially in a time when many voices encourage us to listen to ourselves and to find ourselves, even mature believers can be tempted to forget just who we are in Christ.

In Colossians, the apostle Paul offers such a clear view of how believers are called to think about ourselves as we live *in Christ*. His view is no otherworldly idealism. It is the ultimate realism, which sees Christ clearly and sees everything else in his light, including ourselves.

Throughout their lives, many of our children will have times of struggling with identity. Scripture helps us lift them up in prayer.

For Identity in You

As she follows all the callings your good providence lays out,
please let her understand, amid years full of following,
just who she is as one whom you, O God, have called:
one whose life is hidden with Christ in you.

So help her not to seek for confirmation in the shifting stuff
of sometimes wonderful positions, titles, tasks, or privileges;
lead her, Lord, to set her mind on things above,
where is her home, her life, in Christ her Lord.

May heavenly realities lose their fuzziness
and take on increased clarity through the years,
so in that light she sees the earthly things more clearly,
valuing most of all the Lord who made it all—including her.

When she gives pause, in moments when she stops to ponder,
may she not be searching for herself
among the things that do not last;
may she look up, and see her Lord, and find herself in him.

In midst of life let her not turn from comprehending death,
and may her thoughts turn first to Christ who died for her,
and how in him she died, and in him was given life
that never ends—the resurrection life of Christ our Savior.

Please let her see herself as she is seen by you,
O God in heaven who welcomes us in Christ;
may she look up and far ahead, with joyful hope
of his appearing, when she will appear with him in glory.

Now to him who is able to do far more abundantly than all that we ask or think, according to the power at work within us, to him be glory in the church and in Christ Jesus throughout all generations, forever and ever. Amen. (Eph. 3:20–21)

In asking God to provide even more abundantly than all that we ask or think, may we be seeking his "glory in the church and in Christ Jesus throughout all generations." As we pray for our children, the Bible encourages us to pray that they would live as part of the church and that their lives would bring glory to God in the church, the body of Christ.

Such prayers help us parents take our hands off our adult children's lives, entrusting them more deeply into God's hands and the hands of his people. Jesus is building his church, the eternal family of God; may that family play a central part in our prayers for our children.

Your beautiful bride: see Ephesians 5:25–27; Revelation 19:6–9.

For Love of the Church

I pray that you would keep him planted firm among your
      people,
Lord in heaven who sent your Son to make a people for
      yourself;
let my child through all the passing periods of his life
find family in your church, your body,
your redeemed beloved ones.

Whether he is blessed with family of his own
or your good blessing brings a life of singleness,
may members of the family of God make his way sweet,
and may they help to keep it pointing straight ahead,
as he walks on with saints on every side, toward you.

May he love your church as you do, Lord,
willing to give his life to see your people grow
and prosper, helping them put on the clothes
that you provided for your beautiful bride,
in preparation for the marriage feast to come.

Let him find joy in all that you've created—
in people, places, moments
where you show your hand;
may that joy find full expression
in the gathering of your people,
worshiping around your Word,
seeing you and thanking you together
for your hand of grace on us
in Jesus Christ your Son.

Put on then, as God's chosen ones, holy and beloved, compassionate hearts, kindness, humility, meekness, and patience, bearing with one another and, if one has a complaint against another, forgiving each other; as the Lord has forgiven you, so you also must forgive. And above all these put on love, which binds everything in perfect harmony. (Col. 3:12–14)

If you have time, you might read the whole passage from Colossians 3:1–17—which begins with that upward view of who we are in Christ (vv. 1–4) and then calls believers to "put to death" what does not belong to Christ (vv. 5–9). After that comes this call to "put on" these new clothes. It is worth noting that the "you" addressed here is plural: we God's people do this together, as one body, learning to walk in holiness as a people redeemed by Christ our Savior.

Not only younger people struggle with the old clothes, as we ourselves well know. Sometimes with years comes a letting down of our guard or our self-control. We know well how to pray for our adult children in these matters.

For Habits of Holiness

It takes a lifetime to put on the clothes you give us, Lord,
clothes that look like you, clothes we could never buy
or make or even dream—so beautiful they are.

Thank you that she can put off clothes that fit no longer,
soiled ones, or old and ugly—not right for your child.
Thank you for your Son's death upon the cross, on our behalf,
bearing our sins, our uncleanness, all that is dirty in your sight.
Thank you for covering us with Christ's own righteousness.

Help her take care for how she dresses, Lord—
regularly cleaning out her wardrobe and discarding
sexual impurity, envy, anger, malice, hurtful words,
and all that is not fitting for a redeemed child of you

Help her to join your people in becoming like our Savior,
putting on compassion, kindness, meekness, patience,
and forgiveness modeled after yours—above all, love,
that binds our clothes in perfect harmony.

Dress her in habits of holiness, loving Father.
May she love to put on such fine clothing
given to us in Christ our Lord.

And he gave the apostles, the prophets, the evangelists, the shepherds and teachers, to equip the saints for the work of ministry, for building up the body of Christ, until we all attain to the unity of the faith and of the knowledge of the Son of God. (Eph. 4:11–13)

I love that phrase "to equip the saints"! If we're saints (God's set-apart people, redeemed by Christ), then we're to be equipped for the work of ministry. We all have our various callings of ministry within the body of Christ.

Our children may or may not minister as church leaders or teachers. We can pray according to the Word that, by God's grace, they might keep growing as members of local congregations where they are well equipped to participate in the work of ministry, helping build up the body of Christ.

For Service and Ministry

Let him become a saint who's well equipped, O Lord,
taught and shaped through faithful ministry of other saints
to join the work of ministry among your people,
building up your body, serving faithfully,
aiming without fail for unity according to the Word
and knowledge—lived-out knowledge of the Son of God.

When people look for one who gives himself unselfishly,
not seeking to be served, but quick to serve,
let him come to their minds,
as one resembling Christ the Savior.

When comes a need for help requiring time
and patience, understanding to apply the Word
with Spirit-led discernment, may he come to mind,
as one whose wisdom flows from treasure-stores in Christ.

Let him receive and humbly grow the gifts you've given him;
grant him insight as to how and where to use them best.
May he share his gifts freely, joyfully offering them to you
for others' good and for your glory, never holding back.

Let him be one of many saints so well equipped, O Lord,
that your church may be growing, unified, and strong,
with faithful men and women who belong to Christ
serving and ministering side by side, all for his glory.

David saw that Saul had come out to seek his life. David was in the wilderness of Ziph at Horesh. And Jonathan, Saul's son, rose and went to David at Horesh, and strengthened his hand in God. And he said to him, "Do not fear, for the hand of Saul my father shall not find you. You shall be king over Israel, and I shall be next to you. Saul my father also knows this." And the two of them made a covenant before the LORD. (1 Sam. 23:15–18)

With David and Jonathan, we get a little glimpse into the deepest kind of friendship—between two people who delight to give of themselves to each other, each aiming to encourage and strengthen the other in the Lord. Friendships like this are a great gift, one for which we do well to pray for our children.

We can pray that our children would be open to find blessing—and bring blessing—in all the different levels and kinds of friendships that come their way. May they be ready to be friends who give deeply, self-sacrificially, because they know the greatest Friend, Jesus, who laid down his life for sinners like us.

For Friendships

Let her know friendship, Lord,
with one who knows her heart and soul
and who knows how to strengthen her hand in God.
When she might falter, let her friend speak
words of Jesus—*Do not fear*—and point her
to the promises of God that will not fail.

Give her a friend who will go with her
or come to her in an ordinary day of life
or in a time of looking life and death full in the face.
Let her friend turn her thoughts toward the King—
the King of heaven, Jesus, Lord of all;
let them together bow before King Jesus.

As she befriends the ones you give her, on her way,
she'll never know or be the friend that Jesus is—
perfect friend for sinners like us
who do not know well how to lay our lives down,
especially for those whose heart and soul we know
and know to be sin-stained and broken, just like ours.

But as she knows her Savior, more and more,
please let her be a friend like him,
giving freely of what's rightfully her own,
loving when her love is not deserved,
strengthening a friend's hand in God.

So may friendship shape and fit her soul for heaven
and for her heavenly King.

Continue steadfastly in prayer, being watchful in it with thanksgiving. (Col. 4:2)

As we pray for our children's prayers, we're inevitably praying for our own as well. We understand the challenge of steadfast prayer. I don't know anyone, even among the most wise and godly, who says they've found it easy to learn the discipline of regular prayer and communion with God.

We know the challenge, and we also know what's at stake in this amazing communion with God offered to us in Christ. This is how we draw near to God. This is part of how he grows us and uses us by his Spirit. We long for this, and we long for it for our children.

But we also know the joy of prayer. We know the joy of being close to God. We know the joy of joining with brothers and sisters in prayer before God's throne. We begin to long for this regularly—and we long for it, and pray for it, for our children.

Who helps us by interceding for us: see Romans 8:26–27.

For a Heart to Pray

It is a long, a lifelong watch, O Lord;
please make him steadfast in his communion with you.
May he be watchful, guarding first against an easy pretense
that he knows you intimately; let him come to you with words,
true words that echo yours, and that speak straight
what's in his heart.

As he brings words, let him take care to look and see
the One before whose throne he comes; may he take time
to worship you, to give you praise for who you are,
to confess sins with broken, contrite heart,
to offer thanks for what you've done for needy sinners
through the death and resurrection of your Son.
May he sometimes not progress beyond thanksgiving,
overwhelmed by you, our holy, merciful God.

May his thanksgiving flavor his petitions;
may he ask or even plead with a submissive heart
that is not done with gratefulness for grace outpoured.
When he does ask, Lord, may he lean upon your Spirit's help,
your Spirit who dwells in us followers of you, and who helps us
by interceding for us, perfectly, according to your will.

May he take heart through prayers of folks of faith around him,
brothers, sisters, in your body, who in every prayer of theirs
lead him in prayer, as he leads them—
and so we saints hold one another up, as we walk on.
May fellowship of saints in prayer be dear and dearer to him,
as he grows in fellowship with you his Lord.

But godliness with contentment is great gain, for we brought nothing into the world, and we cannot take anything out of the world. But if we have food and clothing, with these we will be content. But those who desire to be rich fall into temptation, into a snare, into many senseless and harmful desires that plunge people into ruin and destruction. For the love of money is a root of all kinds of evils. It is through this craving that some have wandered away from the faith and pierced themselves with many pangs. (1 Tim. 6:6–10)

So many of these prayers overlap. We can't pray about money, for example, without praying for faith to see beyond the material or without praying to listen carefully to the Scriptures, which speak often about money. Money issues connect to heart issues.

In these verses about money, the apostle Paul uses many words relating to matters of the heart: *contentment, desires, love, craving.* We can pray for our children in all sorts of practical matters relating to money, and we should, but this passage reminds us to pray for their heart attitude toward money—which is directly related to their heart attitude toward the Lord Jesus.

Although he was rich: see 2 Corinthians 8:9.

For Money Matters

Whether she be rich or poor in this world's eyes, Lord,
may she aim for gain that comes by godliness with contentment.

May she bear in heart and mind the Lord our Savior, Jesus
       Christ,
who, although he was rich, became the poorest of us all,
that by his poverty we could be rich, in him.

May she see her money and her worldly goods as gifts from you
for a set time, to steward well,
under your gaze, and for your purposes.

May she be ready to give, and able to receive, if need be,
knowing she brought nothing into this world,
and takes nothing out.

May money from her hand never bring ruin or regret,
but rather help, and often joy—
for Jesus's sake and lifting up his name.

May she give faithfully, needing no public show,
to her own church and ministry, which she knows well,
and to which she gives time and prayer, along with money.

As her life is knit with family, friends, community,
may money never cause division or strife;
may honesty, unselfishness, and liberality rule.

May love of money have no root in her,
but only love of you, O God of grace.

If anyone is not willing to work, let him not eat. For we hear that some among you walk in idleness, not busy at work, but busybodies. Now such persons we command and encourage in the Lord Jesus Christ to do their work quietly and to earn their own living. (2 Thess. 3:10–12)

Commit your work to the LORD,
and your plans will be established. (Prov. 16:3)

It's likely that we will see our children progress through a series of variously combined roles and jobs through the years. May we encourage them well at every point, praying not just for good fruit from diligent work but also for joy in the Lord as they work.

My parents and parents-in-law were especially good at this, always open to their children's sometimes unexpected changes in jobs and plans and places—and always themselves providing an example of relishing their own changing stages of work. We parents have an opportunity to go before our children and show them the joy of thankful, wholehearted work, all the way to the end. Most of all, we parents have an opportunity to pray and commit our work, and our children's work, to the Lord.

For Ongoing Work

Give him a heart to work, O God whose work,
beginning in creation, we do see and wonder at, and imitate
as best we can, displaying your image in us often faintly, Lord,
but with increasing power and clarity
only through the saving work of our Redeemer,
Jesus Christ your Son.

May my child know the joy of being transformed
into the image of your Son, by faith in him
and trusting in his death and resurrection
for new life, and life abundant, full of work that pleases you.

In all his callings, may he labor diligently,
knowing your eye on him from heaven,
and your hand of providence establishing his steps.
May he work well, rest well, and with joy
relish and share the fruit of faithful labor.

If his formal times of labor end,
through sickness or age, according to his plans, or not,
may he still commit the work of all his life to you,
never living in or loving idleness, but with an undivided heart
following this day's calling, aiming as he's always aimed
for Jesus to be known and worshiped
in all corners of the earth—
his own corner, and every corner he can reach,
laboring in prayer and other kinds of work you put before him
to the end.

Think over what I say, for the Lord will give you understanding in everything. (2 Tim. 2:7)

What a gift—the gift of minds to process thoughts and to grow in knowledge and understanding. We know as parents that each child has unique, God-given gifts and abilities to think and learn. We also know that "head knowledge" connects with "heart knowledge"; human beings *know* with their whole beings.

Prayers for the health and growth of our children's minds often begin energetically in earlier years, as our children are educated, but such prayers don't lose their urgency. Let's pray that our grown children might have clarity and patience to think carefully through the words offered by those around them. Let's pray most of all that the Holy Spirit would help them cultivate the godly wisdom and understanding that come from the Lord through his Word, as we come to know Jesus Christ the living Word.

Quick to hear and slow to speak: see James 1:19. *Whose thoughts are high above our thoughts:* see Isaiah 55:9.

For a Mind Alive

Thank you, Lord, for your creation of us human beings
in your image, made to use our minds to understand,
to learn, to ponder, and to grow in knowing you.
I praise you for a child with her own set of intellectual gifts,
according to your personally tailored plan to bless and use her
for your glory and her good.

Help her, I pray, through all her years, to use and grow her mind
as a most gracious gift from you to her.
May she take in your Word with care and let it shape her
        thinking;
may she come to know well the Savior there revealed;
may she take time to meditate and pray for understanding;
may she guard all her thoughts and turn from evil ones,
as your own Spirit helps her and protects her.

Help her consider words around her with discernment,
all in light of your inspired Word;
may she be quick to hear and slow to speak—
but may her measured tongue accompany a mind alive
and aiming with your help for careful thought and
        understanding.

Please keep her, Lord, from falling into habits
of empty hours, of boredom or of entertainment
that would simply numb or dull her mind's imaginings.
Let what is beautiful and true awake her thoughts
and her imagination, to consider you, eternal triune God,
whose thoughts are high above our thoughts,
and whose glory all your children will forever study and sing.

One generation shall commend your works to another,
and shall declare your mighty acts. (Ps. 145:4)

We human beings are all teachers, in one way or another, whether we acknowledge it or not. In raising our children, we parents taught them many things, some intentionally and some unintentionally. Our children will be teachers of all kinds; we can pray that they would be faithful passers-on of the faith, as the psalmist is talking about in Psalm 145. We can pray that they will declare clearly the "mighty acts" of God in sending his own Son to accomplish our salvation through his death on the cross and his resurrection from the grave.

We didn't do it perfectly, and neither will our children. By God's grace, they will do it better! It is an urgent need, not just in biological families but in the church family, for one generation of believers to "commend God's works" to the next— humbly, clearly, lovingly, intentionally.

Flow and overflow like living water: see John 4:13–14.

For a Teaching Heart

Grow in him faith and knowledge of you
that overflows to those ready to learn,
ones he is able to encourage and instruct,
as he commends your works to them, O God,
and passes on your faithfulness
fully revealed to us in Jesus Christ your Son.

Let him not hoard the store of wisdom
you by grace allow him to enjoy;
let him not overestimate his store,
but let him not judge it small,
when it is given by your hand.

Let him not look for large, impressive audiences;
if they come, may he speak humbly, clearly, truly.
Let him develop keenest eyes for individuals near and far—
in the family, in the church, in his city, across the globe—
who need to learn the Word
from one who's learned to know and love the Savior.

O Father God, give him a teaching heart
that longs for others to know you, and know you well.
Let his faith and knowledge never strut, as on a stage,
but rather flow and overflow like living water
shared from the abundance of your Spirit,
for the glory of your Son.

But this is the one to whom I will look:
he who is humble and contrite in spirit
and trembles at my word. (Isa. 66:2)

There's not anything much more basic to pray for our children than for their heart attitude toward God—specifically, that they might come to him in humility, acknowledging their utter dependence, their sin, their reverence and readiness to hear his words to them. The Holy Spirit regenerates hearts to come humbly to the Lord and be saved through faith in Christ; that same Spirit uses God's Word to keep softening our hearts and turning them toward God who has saved us in Christ.

We cannot see into our children's hearts; indeed, they are responsible for their own hearts before God. But what a comfort that we can pray for them, that they would be among the humble and contrite ones who tremble at God's Word.

For Humility

Look on my child as she walks on, Lord God,
and, when you look, I pray you find
a humble heart, a contrite spirit,
one who trembles at your Word.

I pray that all she builds, both visible and invisible,
will not lead her to stand back and admire
what she has built by her own hand,
forgetting the Lord's hand that made all things.

May thankfulness for your great mercy, Lord,
upon her sinful heart,
chase prideful thoughts away;
let her rest not in her own goodness, but in Christ's.

May she not simply know your Word
but keep on bowing low to take it in,
as your own Spirit plants it deep
and lets her grasp your grace, poured out in your own Son.

May she lead many to follow in your way,
but as she leads, may she not grasp for admiration;
let her see herself as seen by you her loving Savior,
let her point her followers far beyond herself, to you.

Please keep her humble, Lord, even as you make her wise,
with wisdom that begins and ends with trembling fear of you—
a trembling full of awe and reverence, as she hears your Word,
a trembling full of love and joy, as she belongs to you, Lord God.

Is anyone among you suffering? Let him pray. Is anyone cheerful? Let him sing praise. Is anyone among you sick? Let him call for the elders of the church, and let them pray over him, anointing him with oil in the name of the Lord. And the prayer of faith will save the one who is sick, and the Lord will raise him up. And if he has committed sins, he will be forgiven. Therefore, confess your sins to one another and pray for one another, that you may be healed. The prayer of a righteous person has great power as it is working. (James 5:13–16)

I don't think it ever becomes easier to see your child suffering, whether he or she is young or old. It's simply a part of yourself hurting. I watched my parents in their eighties watch my older sister suffer and die of a brain disease in her fifties. Their suffering for their child was immeasurable. Such suffering gives us a glimpse into the heart of our Father in heaven.

And yet in the midst of it, my parents prayed, and they remembered to whom they were praying. They knew the Lord is good and sovereign and merciful and present with his children, working his purposes that are greater than we can fathom. When they needed help praying, others helped them. They were helped, and so was my sister, as they all drew near to the throne of grace and found mercy and "grace to help in time of need" (Heb. 4:16).

For Faith in Suffering

When suffering comes, O God, may he see more than suffering.
May he see you at work, and your own hand that reaches down
to lay his path, and hold his soul, and show your glory
to the people and the angels watching all around.

May he look deep into your Word, to find your purposes
revealed in Christ our Savior, from beginning to end;
may he know that he is taking part in your redemptive story;
may he pray to you, surrounded by your praying church.

As he in suffering seeks your face, let him give witness
to those gathered round that he acknowledges your grace;
let him confess his sins, and give thanks publicly
for Jesus's death upon the cross,
and your forgiveness, purchased by the blood of your own Son.

I pray that you would comfort him in his suffering,
and bring his suffering to an end, Lord, as you will.
May you grant strength to persevere,
and may this suffering take its place as a good chapter
in your story of grace.

Let many watching ones learn more about the story;
let them search and find the Savior at its heart—
your glorious Son who came down low and suffered for us,
that, through the gift of faith in him,
our sin-sick suffering might finally end.

But love your enemies, and do good, and lend, expecting nothing in return, and your reward will be great, and you will be sons of the Most High, for he is kind to the ungrateful and the evil. Be merciful, even as your Father is merciful. (Luke 6:35–36)

We may have tried to the best of our ability to teach mercy to our children; in the end, it is God who shows and teaches mercy to all of us his children. Often, our children show mercy in ways we might never have imagined; in their adult years particularly, as their paths take them places we've never been, our children can help teach us about the merciful heart of God. How wonderful, to witness the flow of God's never-ending mercy.

And so we keep praying to our merciful Father in heaven that his children might be merciful, even as he is merciful.

Final wrath withheld: see 2 Peter 3:9. *In him you give us all things*: see Romans 8:31–32.

For a Heart of Mercy

May she love her enemies, may she do good,
and may she lend, expecting nothing in return.

> Father, you have shown us how to love unlovely ones,
> in your forgiveness and redemption, through your Son,
> of sinners like me, with nothing in my hand to bring you.

May she be kind to the ungrateful and the evil,
putting down the hate or anger that wells up inside.

> Father, you are kind to those you've made,
> with blessings poured out generously on your earth,
> and final wrath withheld, while many come to faith in Jesus.

May her generosity and kindness flow from a merciful heart,
the transformed heart you give your children, through your Son.

> Father, you are merciful.
> You do not give us that which we deserve;
> instead, you gave your only Son, to bear your wrath for us,
> and in him you give us all things.

May she be merciful, as you, Father, are merciful.

I hate, I despise your feasts,
  and I take no delight in your solemn assemblies. . . .
But let justice roll down like waters,
  and righteousness like an ever-flowing stream.
    (Amos 5:21, 24)

But woe to you Pharisees! For you tithe mint and rue and every herb, and neglect justice and the love of God. These you ought to have done, without neglecting the others. (Luke 11:42)

The Bible teaches us what to hate and what to love—that is, what God hates and what God loves. And it's clear that God hates empty ritual, religious show from those who are neglecting "justice and the love of God."

There is injustice all around us, near and far—abused and downtrodden and murdered human beings who were created in God's image. Let us pray that our children (and we) will not turn away to our own comfort or self-justification but will give ourselves to that amazing combination of "justice and the love of God." To understand how these two go together, we will have to keep going back to the cross.

For Practicing Justice

Lord, let him hate a righteous show,
first in himself,
knowing you want justice and the love of God.
Let him not neglect the cultivating of a heart of love
for you, who loved him first,
and with that heart, a life that shows your love
in practicing your justice.

Please let him revel in your justice—
first the justice you showed at the cross where Jesus died
bearing your just wrath for sin, for sinners' sake,
and showing the extent of your amazing love.
May he know as his life's foundation
that Jesus is the Christ, your Son, who died for him,
who rescued him.

May that faith guide him in loving you
and loving others, showing them a God of justice
who sees every sin and will bring perfect justice
for each human being, in the end, and without end.

Now, Lord, on the way to perfect justice,
may he speak and act like you, the one he loves.
May he look for ones who've been downtrodden, overlooked;
may he give energy to rescue others, body and soul—
the vulnerable, weak, discarded, left behind
by ones so busy with providing for themselves.
Let him not join some righteous-looking throng.
Let him help justice to roll down like waters,
and righteousness like an ever-flowing stream.

For God gave us a spirit not of fear but of power and love and self-control. (2 Tim. 1:7)

We may not always know when and why our grown children are afraid; sometimes adults are good at covering up fears. We don't need to know; we can pray for our children in their fears, which they will certainly face throughout their lives. We can ask God to give them the "power and love and self-control" that come from the risen Lord himself, by his Spirit.

This prayer, like so many others, asks God to bring round our children the fellowship of God's people, the very body of Christ. It is a comfort to know that more people than us parents are praying for and with our children. We are also then spurred on to pray faithfully for and with those in the congregations around us. We're all praying for and with many people's children.

The witness of your Spirit with her spirit: see Romans 8:16.

For Facing Fears

Lord God, whether her body is strong or weak,
please let her inner self be fortified by you;
may that same Spirit whom you send to draw us to yourself
fill her, sustain her, give her power and love and self-control.

I pray you would send loving ones around her
who can help to lift her up when she would fear or faint;
but when there's no one, let her hear your voice,
through your Word telling her that she can trust in you.

When she's afraid—of pain, of scorn, of harm,
or of the flurry of dark things that threaten and attack
when it is night or she is worn—please let her heed the witness
of your Spirit with her spirit; let her rest as your beloved child.

If she comes to fear some persecution for her faith in you,
if she or one she loves is called to suffer for your name,
please let her know and trust the power of your Spirit
not just in her alone, but in your people, in the body of Christ.

Let her think much on Christ who suffered and died,
bearing our sins, and on his resurrection from the grave;
seeing him risen, there at your right hand, O Father,
let her meet fear with resurrection power and love.

The simple believes everything,
  but the prudent gives thought to his steps.
One who is wise is cautious and turns away from evil,
  but a fool is reckless and careless. (Prov. 14:15–16)

I imagine most of us could tell stories of adults we know (perhaps including ourselves) who have hurt others (and themselves) through their lack of prudence and self-control in dealing with technology—whether in matters of money, or sex, or time, or perhaps communications that were thoughtless or untrue.

Technology's power for good is a given, and we should pray that our children are ones who harness this good in ways that will help and encourage many. The role of technology in sending out gospel truth and connecting believers in all corners of the world is astounding and exciting.

It's not surprising that such dramatic good has such dramatic potential for evil. Of course, the evil is in human hearts, not in technology. Technology just seems to give evil an open door—especially for one lacking in prudence and self-control. And so we continue to pray for our children, asking the Lord to deliver them from evil and, by his Spirit and his Word, to help them give thought to their steps.

One of your beloved sheep: see John 10:14–16.

For Wisdom in Cyberspace

Prudence day by day, Lord, I would pray for him;
help him to grow, not lessen, in his self-control,
as the years grow; may he give careful thought
to every step, when walking on an unknown path
or one he thinks that he knows well by now.
Please, by your Spirit and your people and your Word,
keep growing in him wisdom, caution, sober-mindedness
that turn him from the highway of the fool,
where recklessness and carelessness steer lives away from you.

Make him no believer in the many words and pictures
regularly calling from that screen in front of him,
on desk, or table, or in his hand, at work, at home;
help him discern and value what is good and true;
help him disbelieve and hate what's false,
whether it be promises of comfort and prosperity,
or temptations of pleasure to be privately enjoyed,
or tasty morsels of slander sent out for many to chew,
or simply foolishness that numbs and dumbs the mind.

Make him a true believer in you, Lord,
a faithful follower of Christ his Savior,
one of your beloved sheep
who knows and hears your voice among the many others.
Let his ears become attuned to the Good Shepherd's voice.
Please help him turn away from evil;
let him help others turn from evil, turn to you,
and walk with prudence on the good path of the wise.

May the God of hope fill you with all joy and peace in believing, so that by the power of the Holy Spirit you may abound in hope. (Rom. 15:13)

Some people get a little grumpy, less joyful, as they get older. Don't you think it's a matter of what we dream of and hope for? The passing of years limits our hopes and dreams—unless those hopes and dreams are tethered to something eternal.

I love to pray about all the things my children are hoping for, little or big, temporary or eternal. But it's the eternal things that are tethered to this "God of hope" the apostle Paul is talking about. It's the eternal hopes that grow not more limited with years but actually more clear—the hope of the resurrection, for example, through Christ our Lord.

Let's pray that the God of hope will increasingly fill our children with joy as the years pass.

For a Joyful Heart

Let her abound in hope, O God of hope,
as you fill her with joy and peace
that grow not from a lack of struggle
but from the power of the Holy Spirit
dwelling in ones who believe,
by grace alone, through faith alone
in your own Son, who died and rose again,
a spotless sacrifice for all our sins.

Father God, may you grant joy and peace
as she believes in you—even more deeply
through the afflictions you ordain—
for you are with her,
and through the power of your Spirit
you transform my child into the image of your Son.

If her life is filled with many good things—
loved ones loving back, much comfort, pleasure, fruitful work—
please grant the deepest joy as well;
may she not let the good gifts from your hand
turn her attention from the greatest gift
that gives her lasting joy, along with all those who believe.

May her joy be evident, winsome;
may it fill a room she enters
like a scent of something lovely one would like to find and keep.
Let her with passing time not let her soul slump down
but rather grow and strengthen with increased joy,
joy in believing, joy from you.

I wish that all were as I myself am. But each has his own gift from God, one of one kind and one of another. . . .

I want you to be free from anxieties. The unmarried man is anxious about the things of the Lord, how to please the Lord. But the married man is anxious about worldly things, how to please his wife, and his interests are divided. And the unmarried or betrothed woman is anxious about the things of the Lord, how to be holy in body and spirit. But the married woman is anxious about worldly things, how to please her husband. I say this for your own benefit, not to lay any restraint upon you, but to promote good order and to secure your undivided devotion to the Lord. (1 Cor. 7:7, 32–35)

The apostle Paul is happy to be single—and he tells the Corinthian believers why! Now, he elsewhere teaches about the good of marriage. But it is important to hear his voice on singleness as a good thing as well, a certain kind of gift from God to be used for gospel purposes in these last days before Christ comes again.

Many parents I know (and I myself) have prayed for unmarried grown children and asked the Lord to give them the gift of marriage—in particular when the grown children themselves desire this gift. These verses challenge us to pray as well that, as long as the gift of singleness may belong to one of our children, he or she might treasure that gift and use it with "undivided devotion to the Lord."

Your commission to go: see Matthew 28:19–20.

For Thankfulness in Singleness

For your gift of singleness to him right now
I thank you, Lord, and pray he might receive this gift
with thankfulness, using this gift to please you,
giving back to you the gifts you've given.
May he devote his heart to knowing you
and serving you and building up your people,
in the time you give us now, before Christ comes again.

May he rightly value freedom from anxieties
that come with marriage, family;
help him use this freedom with his eyes on you,
with joy, with self-control, with discipline
that sets him free to know and share your Word.
May he have wisdom, strength, and time to minister
to one in trouble, one who needs the presence
of a faithful one not just through prayer, but in the flesh.

If he be anxious, Lord, let him be anxious
for the things of you—your call to holiness, in Christ;
your commission to go and make disciples of all nations;
your clear warning that the time is short,
before Christ comes again.

Give him an undivided heart, O Father God;
in all his longings, may he learn to long for you,
and find you, as he hides your Word deep in his heart
and trusts you to meet every longing, finally,
through your everlasting grace to him, in Christ.

"Therefore a man shall leave his father and mother and hold fast to his wife, and the two shall become one flesh." This mystery is profound, and I am saying that it refers to Christ and the church. (Eph. 5:31–32; see also Gen. 2:24)

As we pray for our married children, we have two in one to pray for! It feels good to enlarge our hearts and enlarge our family.

Ephesians 5:32 is a kind of landmark verse concerning marriage, often quoted because it says so clearly what God from the beginning intended marriage to be: a picture of Christ and the church. But this clear statement is not simple; it expresses a profound mystery.

The surrounding verses explain a lot, but it's still a great mystery, this union that happens in a marriage and that points to the ultimate spiritual union of Christ and the church he loves, for whom he laid down his life. What a magnificent prayer for our married children, in all the ebbs and flows of married joys and sorrows: that they would understand more and more, and live out more and more, the spiritual reality of Christ and the church.

The marriage supper of the Lamb: see Revelation 19:6–9.

For Blessing in Marriage

For your gift of marriage to my child, I thank you, Lord,
and pray this gift will bring long-lasting joy and fruit
both in the lives of husband and wife
and in the myriad lives they touch.
May the reality of Christ and his beloved church
be ever clearer to them as they live the picture of it
through the covenant of marriage ordained by you
to bless us humans, and to show yourself to us.

In ordinary days, or days of tension, or of happiness,
give them hearts to ponder what a mystery they're living—
not seeing it yet, and longing still to see,
but by your grace together holding fast the promise
of the marriage supper of the Lamb,
when those redeemed by the Lamb's blood
will be invited, dressed as a bride in shining clothes,
to join the feast, rejoice, and give him glory.

May that hope light up their married days,
helping heal the hurts that need forgiving,
giving substance to their marriage vows,
as by your grace they're bringing home
the very love of Christ, who gave his life for us.

May joy grow from that hope;
may their home be freshened with the air of joy
that draws in many, young and old, who breathe in life
and who can see a bit more clearly, in this husband and wife,
the Lord's amazing love for us.

As a father shows compassion to his children,
*so the L*ORD *shows compassion to those who fear him.*
For he knows our frame;
he remembers that we are dust. (Ps. 103:13–14)

It is a privilege to pray for our children as they long for children of their own. Sometimes they share with us their longing; sometimes we guess; always we have to measure our words in speaking with them about it; and always we can take these petitions to a heavenly Father whom we can trust completely as we pray.

It's a prayer that moves our parent hearts. Even if we ourselves never experienced the pain of waiting and longing, we as parents understand the intensity of the desire and the blessedness of the gift of a child.

In these prayers of longing and waiting, there is the blessing of coming close to God who is the sovereign source of all life. Even as we pray for an answer to our children's prayer, we can pray, too, that they would in the process draw near to their compassionate heavenly Father.

You created the first human from the dust: see Genesis 2:7.

For Faithful Longing for a Child

Lord, I thank you that you hear my child's prayers
of longing for a child—the gift you call a heritage, a blessing,
but a gift that in your providence you now withhold.

May this longing wife and husband know your kindness,
your compassion, as they ask, and ask.
May they in asking look full in your face,
dig deeply in your Word,
and see your steadfast love for us your children.
You, O Father, know our frame; you remember we are dust,
for you created the first human from the dust upon the ground.
You are the Lord of life. We've nowhere else to go.

Father God, I as a parent bow down low before your throne,
and see I do not understand your ways, so high they are.
Help me to trust; help me to pray with eyes on you;
help me to say no more than I should say to anyone but you;
help me, and help my child to know your gifts to us are perfect,
better than we ever could imagine in our strength alone.

Bless the home they're building; may their firm foundation rest
on your unfailing love, O God who gave your only Son to
        save us.
Dig out depths of faith within their hearts, I pray;
fill the space of longing with the joy of your own presence.
Guard their marriage; bring and keep them close to you,
and closer, as they seek your face.
And, if it be your will, may they welcome a child.

In the waiting, thank you that you hear our prayers
from us your children, trusting in our heavenly Father.

Hear, O Israel: The LORD our God, the LORD is one. You shall love the LORD your God with all your heart and with all your soul and with all your might. And these words that I command you today shall be on your heart. You shall teach them diligently to your children, and shall talk of them when you sit in your house, and when you walk by the way, and when you lie down, and when you rise. You shall bind them as a sign on your hand, and they shall be as frontlets between your eyes. You shall write them on the doorposts of your house and on your gates. (Deut. 6:4–9)

Grandparenting! That's another entire book! The focus here is on praying for our children as parents—and we know from personal experience how much they need our prayers (more than our advice).

Sometimes we get to be close and personally involved in our grandchildren's lives; sometimes we don't, for various reasons. In any and every case, we can pray—for the grandchildren and for our children who are their parents. We can pray.

Let's pray that our children would introduce their children to the Lord Jesus, day by day—in their own homes and in the fellowship of God's people. Let's pray that our children would show God's love in Christ Jesus and that his Word would be on their lips continually. Let's pray all the prayers we've prayed before, but this time with the next generation in view! May God grant our children grace to keep passing it on.

For Grace in Parenting

Father, what a gift you've given to my child,
to become the parent of a child. How I wonder at your grace
that keeps on flowing, generation after generation.
This I pray: that mother and father both,
as long as you allow your gift of life and breath,
would show your love to their beloved child.

May they delight to lead this child in following you,
even as the path ahead winds through a tumultuous world.
May they learn and teach and draw upon your Word
as the unfailing wellspring of their hope.
May Jesus Christ, his death, his resurrection,
his promise of new life for all who trust in him,
be daily spoken, lived, and taught from all the Scriptures;
night and day, in coming and in going, may your Word
so fill these parents' hearts and minds that it must spill
into the heart and mind of this young life.

May they trust you, loving Father, with their child,
taking utmost care and yet not giving way to anxiousness
or fear for daily hurdles or for thoughts of all that is to come.
May they be regularly thankful, joyful, for your presence with
        them,
most of all for your unending grace in Jesus Christ your Son.

Lord God on high, I thank you for the avenue of prayer
through which I pour out words of praise, and yearnings, all.
Give me a guarded, gracious tongue with these grown children
who will carry on their parenting all by your grace,
and, I would pray, with many of their own prayers to you,
in Jesus's name.

Now the LORD *said to Abram, "Go from your country and your kindred and your father's house to the land that I will show you. And I will make of you a great nation, and I will bless you and make your name great, so that you will be a blessing. I will bless those who bless you, and him who dishonors you I will curse, and in you all the families of the earth shall be blessed." (Gen. 12:1–3)*

Everyone's extended family gatherings are unique. But as parents of adult children, we may well share the experience of periodically coming together with family in growing and changing configurations—which can often be wonderful *and* which can sometimes feel strange or tense.

These gatherings stretch our hearts in challenging ways, and they stretch our prayers. We learn better what we've always known: that our immediate family is not just for ourselves; it is part of God's big plan to bless many, many families for the glory of Jesus.

For Family Gatherings

Heavenly Father, would you bless our family gatherings,
perhaps in summer, or at holidays, or often,
as we come together with the family you've given us—
a varied assortment of grandparents, parents, spouses,
children and grandchildren, siblings, cousins, friends.
You have joined us, shaped us; first, I thank you
for the privilege and pain and joy, all mixed,
of seeing your hand of providence in this my family.

I pray first that not one person gathered, young or old,
will have come and gone not having heard
clear witness from at least one mouth, or many more,
to the grace of God in Christ who is our life,
who died for sinners, who arose, who is our living hope.
May Jesus Christ be named and praised among us.
May his love be strong among us, even in our weaknesses.
May we speak with gracious words, the words of truth in love.

As I'm praying for my child, or for my children, Lord,
I see that my prayers grow, and grow to cover like a tent
all the connected lives that come together in our gathering.
May my prayers grow; indeed, may my heart grow,
and may it become more like yours, O God,
who loves and blesses each of us your many children
with an endless and unfailing love, in Christ your Son.

May the child or children that by grace you give me
spread your grace to generations still to come,
finding joy not only in an earthly family now, O Lord,
but in the family you are gathering, in Christ, for all eternity.

But the path of the righteous is like the light of dawn,
which shines brighter and brighter until full day.
(Prov. 4:18)

Our adult children do age before our eyes, hard as it is to realize. We parents have always been the older ones. But there's that gray hair on my son's head or the wrinkles that my daughter is suddenly noticing . . .

What grace we can share with our children as we face aging without fear; as we laugh together; as we sometimes cry together; as we refuse to pretend we are other than we are; as we call a middle-aged or older face beautiful; as we pray to age with gospel hope, knowing with utter certainty that one day these bodies will be resurrected and made perfect forever, all because of our resurrected Savior, the Lord Jesus Christ.

Proverbs would lead us to pray that our children (and we) would walk the path of faith that becomes not darker but brighter until full day.

For Clear-Sighted Aging

I'm praying to age with grace myself, O Lord,
but here's another thing again: to pray for my child's aging.
I'm amazed (and thankful) to be here and old enough
to see her growing older, following the path you've given
as it leads her into years where suddenly she finds
that others think her older—
and that she's indeed no longer young.

Give her your eyes to see her path, O sovereign Lord;
let her look back and find a long, clear trail of grace;
let her look forward and find not just shadows
but a growing light—the light of Jesus's face.

Now, may she face straight the truths of bodies aging;
may she exercise and steward well her strength,
while never aiming to pretend that she is young.
May she hate the enemy that is death,
but may she walk ahead in faith that death is conquered,
through the death and resurrection of your Son.

May she with a light heart walk toward the light,
hoping in no goodness of her own,
but in the righteousness of Christ her Savior,
who in his rising from the grave
lights up her path with resurrection hope.

May her path indeed be like the light of dawn,
which shines brighter and brighter until full day.

> *The LORD is my rock and my fortress and my deliverer,*
>   *my God, my rock, in whom I take refuge,*
>   *my shield, and the horn of my salvation, my stronghold....*
> *In my distress I called upon the LORD;*
>   *to my God I cried for help.*
> *From his temple he heard my voice,*
>   *and my cry to him reached his ears. (Ps. 18:2, 6)*

The Psalms mark out such deep and well-worn paths of lament for a troubled soul, all leading to the Lord himself in whom we take refuge. Many of us have followed those paths, by God's grace, and knowing them helps us pray for our children in their times of trouble—that they, too, would cry to God for help and find him to be their fortress and their deliverer.

In light of all the Scriptures, we know the ultimate deliverer and can pray that our children would call upon the name of the Lord Jesus, trusting him for salvation and for a refuge that cannot be taken away.

Who bore our sins in his own body: see 1 Peter 2:24. *Lifts his drooping hands*: see Hebrews 12:12–13.

For Help in Trouble

In his distress, O Lord, let him be quick to call on you.
May he come into your presence trusting in your Son
for his salvation, laying all his sins on Jesus,
who bore our sins in his own body on the tree,
so we by grace, through faith, might be set free.

When he is troubled, low in spirit, may he cry to you for help,
and may he know that his cry reaches to your ears.
If he is battling doubt, or darkness in his soul,
may he have ears to hear your Word,
and may he speak it back to you in faith;
even in darkness may he find the rock, the refuge
that is you, O Lord, the God of our salvation.

Let him not stop, along the path you put before him,
though the middle parts sometimes seem long, or slippery,
and then later can come steep and treacherous descents.
But let him walk in faith that lights his eyes to see ahead
and lifts his drooping hands, strengthens his weak knees,
so that his feet can follow straight the path that leads to life.
May he find brothers, sisters, walking with him on that path,
ones who cry out with him, and walk with him in faith,
speaking your Word, and following the Savior.

In his distress, O Lord, let him be quick to call on you,
his rock, his fortress, his deliverer, to the end.

And beginning with Moses and all the Prophets, he interpreted to them in all the Scriptures the things concerning himself. (Luke 24:27)

Many people have read Luke 24 and wished they could have been there on the road to Emmaus along with those two disciples as they got to hear Jesus teach them from all the Scriptures concerning himself. They got a personal lesson in the story line of the Bible—from the main character of the story.

We have received the completed Scriptures, telling us the story of Jesus from beginning to end. We can hold all the words in our hands. How rich we are! And how rich are our children!

Let's pray that the words of Scripture, from beginning to end, will increasingly shape the minds and thoughts of our children.

For Word-Shaped Thoughts

Let her think on your creation of the world, and Adam—
the first Adam who from such a place of goodness fell so low
and in whom all since him have fallen.
Let her wonder at the promise of a seed,
the One appointed to bruise Satan's head.
Let her reflect on Noah and the flood,
on your strong hand of judgment, and of grace.
Let her consider Abraham,
and your sure promise of great blessing to his seed
and through his seed to all the families of the earth.
Let her contemplate your steadfast love and faithfulness
as you did grow that seed into a people,
who received your law through Moses your appointed prophet
and who grew to be a shining nation, ruled by David,
who so gloriously gave his people prayers and praises
and to whom you gave the promise of a king eternal on his
            throne.
Let her ponder how the promised king for centuries was
            longed for
by your sin-sick people so in need of a Redeemer—
who at your appointed time appeared, the Word made flesh,
the second Adam, promised seed, your Son our Savior,
King from heaven come to save his people from their sins.
Let her fix her soul's eyes on Jesus Christ who died, who rose,
who promised he will build his church
and finally come again to judge the earth
and dwell with us his people
in a heaven and earth made new.

May your Word shape her thoughts, O Lord,
all to the praise and glory of Jesus.

He is the image of the invisible God, the firstborn of all creation. For by him all things were created, in heaven and on earth, visible and invisible, whether thrones or dominions or rulers or authorities—all things were created through him and for him. And he is before all things, and in him all things hold together. And he is the head of the body, the church. He is the beginning, the firstborn from the dead, that in everything he might be preeminent. For in him all the fullness of God was pleased to dwell, and through him to reconcile to himself all things, whether on earth or in heaven, making peace by the blood of his cross. (Col. 1:15–20)

In this magnificent "Christ hymn," the apostle Paul is letting us glimpse the glory of just who Jesus is. There is no better final prayer for our children than that they would see Jesus for who he is, think on him, love him, believe in him, and serve him all their days, into eternity.

For My Child to Think on Jesus

Looking back, please let him see your hand, O God.
May he look far, to the creation of all things through your own
        Son—
and let his thoughts stretch farther, to eternity past,
before all things, when your Son dwelled with you in glory.
But then let him look to the incarnation of your Son,
and to the cross, and to the empty tomb;
let his thoughts linger there, at that climax of history
which makes our little histories make sense—
looking to Jesus, Lord of all who came to save us.

Looking to present days and urgencies,
let him remind himself of Jesus,
in whom all things hold together, even now, this day.
Let him consider how our Savior holds the stars in place
and by his will makes human hearts beat, lungs expand.
May he look to Jesus as the head of the church body,
family of saints redeemed—visible now only in part.
May he live in your church as his real home today, O God,
looking to Jesus, Lord whose Spirit lives in us who live in him.

Looking ahead, may he not fear. May he look far
(that is, beyond his plans for this year and the next),
to think on that amazing moment quickly coming
when he sees the face of Jesus, whether when he dies
or when Jesus returns to judge and to make all things new.
Let him in faith consider his inheritance, his home with Christ
our Savior in heaven now, and then in the new heaven and earth,
with all the church singing before his throne. Let him forever
        live
looking to Jesus, Lord who reigns eternally. Amen.

Your steadfast love, O LORD, extends to the heavens,
your faithfulness to the clouds.
Your righteousness is like the mountains of God;
your judgments are like the great deep;
man and beast you save, O LORD.

How precious is your steadfast love, O God!
The children of mankind take refuge in the shadow of
your wings.
They feast on the abundance of your house,
and you give them drink from the river of your delights.
For with you is the fountain of life;
in your light do we see light. (Ps. 36:5–9)

The steadfast love of the Lord is from everlasting to everlasting. Dwelling in his house as his children, we can trust the Lord with our children.

In our parenting, we can rest and hope and delight in God's steadfast love, shown fully and finally in the Lord Jesus Christ.

How precious is your steadfast love, O God!

For My Parent Heart

All I ask you for my child, O Lord,
is all you've given to me, in Christ;
there is no measure of your steadfast love
that reaches to the heavens;
I ask from out of my abundance in knowing you.

In all my asking, let me rest
in your great love and faithfulness;
you are the Father in heaven
who provides a refuge for your children
in the shadow of your wings;
they feast on the abundance of your house;
you give them drink from the river of your delights.
I pray trusting your provision for my child,
for I have tasted just how good is your provision.

My life, and my child's life
are not our own, but gifts from you,
O God, who are yourself the fountain of life.
What grace, that you should give me life
and let me nurture another, given by you.
What most amazing grace,
that you should bring life to a soul that's dead,
through your own Son,
light of the world, the light of life.

I thank you that you call your children, Lord,
to faith in Christ your Son, our Savior,
and to a home where we will feast forever, with you.

Conclusion

As we continue to pray for our grown children, may thanksgiving wind like a recurring melody through our prayers. Thanksgiving is like salt that flavors everything—including our own hearts as we pray. In his letter to the Colossians, the apostle Paul reminds them again and again: be thankful!

> And let the peace of Christ rule in your hearts, to which indeed you were called in one body. And *be thankful*. (Col. 3:15)

> And whatever you do, in word or deed, do everything in the name of the Lord Jesus, *giving thanks* to God the Father through him. (Col. 3:17)

> Continue steadfastly in prayer, being watchful in it *with thanksgiving*. (Col. 4:2)

We will be praying for our children through many sorrows and joys, surely never running out of petitions to make for them as they walk their pathways. May all our petitions be flavored with thanksgiving to God the Father, through our Lord Jesus.

Thank you, Father, for giving us life and breath. Thank you that we can come to you as your children, redeemed by your Son, by grace, through faith. Thank you that you hear our prayers. Thank you for our children. Thank you that we can trust your power and your goodness in the lives of our children. Thank you that you sovereignly lay out all of our paths for your glory. Thank you that you don't ask us or our children to walk alone, but you speak to us in your Word, you give your Spirit to dwell in those who believe, and you make us part of the body of Christ forever.

And on and on! Once we catch the tune called "thanksgiving," we love to sing it. We hum it all the time. It turns our thoughts to Jesus. We learn not to be anxious but to know the peace of coming to the Lord "in everything by prayer and supplication with thanksgiving" (Phil. 4:6).

Perhaps in the final blank pages of this book you will want to write some of your own prayers, bringing your adult children before God's throne of grace—continuing "steadfastly in prayer, being watchful in it with thanksgiving."

Prayers of a Parent

Did you enjoy this book?
Consider leaving a review online.
The author appreciates your feedback!

Or write to P&R at editorial@prpbooks.com
with your comments. We'd love to hear from you.